ENDLESS NIGHT

ENDLESS NIGHT

ASSEM BAZZI

ORNITHOPTER PRESS CHEVY CHASE

First Edition

Published by Ornithopter Press
www.ornithopterpress.com

ISBN 978-1-942723-21-9

Library of Congress Control Number: 2026939479

Cover photograph:
Rust, 2025
by Mark Harris

Design and composition by Mark Harris

Contents

Special thanks to Christiane Raffoul for her help as an un/official agent

ENDLESS NIGHT

The apocalypse is not an event, but a daily occurrence.

A Bed of Spikes with an Uncomfortable Pillow

Nightmares are
Too dramatic.

I dream
Not of pleasant things
I dream of
Minute inconveniences.

Someone not getting out of the doorway
A pebble staying and growing in my left shoe
Meeting faces I don't know with false words of intimacy
My teeth falling out on my way to the dentist
Being able to fly but having problems at liftoff
Kissing a woman that turns into a metallic unripe tomato
Attending an execution with a rusty blade
Having to arrange a funeral with a low-budget plan
Being late to a watch symposium

The days
Inseparable from each other.

I dance
Continuously
To unwelcomed beats
On a slipping dance floor
Atop a deserted altar
Maintained by vines

I wake
To constant Sundays
To a world drudging through cyclical motions
To a world packed to the brim with distractions.

I wake
To a warm beer
In Hell.

Pillow Talk

Bring the bag
  Full of secrets
Lose the shadows
  Weighing your feet
Stash the dirt
  Deep in your pockets

Blind the eyes
Slash the tires
Block your GPS

Never look back

The alleys are your friends
The trash in 'em, your pillows
The naked legs, only in your head

Never look back

Don't give 'em a reason
Don't rush it
Don't make their jobs easier

Bring the bag
  Full of secrets
Open the familiar doors
  Sheltering familiar faces
Close the windows
Close the blinds
Close your eyes
Stay close
Stay hidden

Whisper to me the words
  they would steal from us

Endless Days

It's quiet enough to hear the nicotine leaves burn
It's quiet enough to hear the thoughts you bury
It's quiet enough to hear mosquitoes hovering
It's quiet enough to feel the tick of seconds

No car engine sparks to life
No bakery opens in the early hours
for schoolchildren and construction workers
No bus to take their dejected morning faces
towards another day of… something

A car just went by
Stealing a moment in the forbidden air

There was no war
There was no mass explosion
No claims of heroics or villainy
No theatrics

A humbling silence
Enshrined with empty

Everything before is old
Everything before is on hold

Homes are put to the test
Some are only houses
Adorned with things
Lacking warmth

Others lack any warmth
Dead before
Shunned before
Forgotten long ago

Gas prices are low
Nobody drives

Another car dared to peek its headlights out of its spot
Driving in the sanctity
of the last moments
before the morning light,
hounded on the corners
outside the alleyways,
for good reason

a breath of air is terminal
a touch induces paranoia
a look burns through screens

walking a dog,
in its ignorance,
brings childlike forgetfulness
until the next pair of eyes
bear fear
bear anger
bear hatred
bear anxiety
at your mere presence

Children of god
Make their proclamations
Point their fingers
At the physical
Through their metaphysical
Harboring their hypocrisy
Fascists enjoy their martial laws
Doctors struggle with quiet focus behind their microscopes

Another car swerves by
Its tires and shot brakes are louder than trumpets

But everyone is too fast asleep
To bear witness to the almighty slipping moments
Of trespass

It's quiet enough to hear
The dreams of others
As they linger
Tenderly
Along the windowpanes
Along the cardboards
Above pavements and pillows
Everyone's dream is a single burn away from being heard

It's quiet

Quiet enough to hear the neighbor's pot boiling
On the lowest of heats

Tales are formed
Narratives erupt
To place the world in a pleasing conceivable pattern
Knitted by a storytelling grandmother that wreaks of onions
"Foreign powers conspired"
"The Avenging gods are displeased"
"Mother Nature is harvesting"
"The machinations of the Devil"
"The upper class
    concocting
    biological
    worldwide
    warfare
    on uprisings"

the absurd
too daunting
to be humored

the absurd
too illogical
to comprehend

the absurd
plainly
provides
the fact
that not everything is
under control

The planet heals
-I don't care-
The animals thrive
-I care less-

I yearn for what was
My streets
My cafés
The faces of others I cherish
The stories around them
My challenges
My battles
My life

I hear the birds chipper away
Mocking
I desire a rifle to hunt my breakfast

A motorcycle is heard
Faintly
The rider is careful
-No joyrides-

Projects are made
Distractions iconized

Views Askewed
Priorities shifted
(for the moment)

A stench
Proceeds into
Every nostril

No amount of soap
Is enough
To wash away
The dirt

And tomorrow
Keeps its
Petty pace

Until we can arrive
At a fair game of chess
Safe in our movements against the cloaked player
Having born a collective scar
Having probably learned nothing

Stained

Tear-stained pillow
Harbors the nightmares
Made of illogical timing
Occupied with every face I know
Stacked with invaders propelling my escape

They wake me
With black-stained eyes
In the night-stained world

They Drive me outwards
In a furious quiet pace

My rain-soaked head
Sponges in acidity
Melts away my brain

My feet stain every back-alley and corner
My sanctuary is stained by the shouts of irregulars

I wallow back to my house
Read fantasies stained by boredom

I am allowed sleep
Only as the sun rises
Frustrating me as time expires

But I am armed
With Stains
  that mark my history
  that engrave my failures
  that shield my skin

From the sun
From the morning news

From the words of soberminded lecturers
From my own tears

A Prolonged Epic

As the remnants of wine
Stain the floor and scent of the room
I am seated comfortably on a couch
As others strive to clean the mess

I get up in the morning
Zoom past the news
Till I get bloody cartoons
Where cat and mouse
Survive through mutual violence and trickery

As fast cars of the West zoom by indifferently
I hear the lowly whines of a street dog
That wakes my dad mid-sleep

I don't care for old romanticism
There is no pure soil of motherlands
The olive tree has been turned into concrete
The key was forgotten in a bar, and the door has already been broken through

People are dead and dying
Wars end
We face a prolonged modern Epic
Belonging to a Butcher
Lacking heroes
Stacked with forgotten martyrs
Started by a promise
Kept by building contracts
Sustained by selective memory
Endorsed by bureaucrats of ammunition
Recorded by poetic propaganda
Cheered on by the grieving
Whose tears
are wiped clean
by gunpowder.

Waking up on 68th Street

68th street is sterilized,
by the late night breeze.

There are
No pushers to elucidate the effects of herbs
No wise men to stand guard in front of cafés
No cigarette buds carpeting the road
No youth to straggle behind
No bums to part away from with change and wisdom

Lovers have retreated

Away from this scene
In the refuge of four walls
Away from the wide streets
Under a roof
Away from the doomed celebrations
Embraced by privacy

No one dances but a passing fool
A lonesome figure
Holding a trumpet
Jumping between the sidewalk cracks
Singing in tongues
Ignoring signs with delight
Stumbling with rhythm
Lurking from beneath lamps
Longing for a warm hand
Avoiding sobriety
To the beat of a deadman
To the voice of a junky
To the memory of a secret, shared beneath blankets
Feet liberated
Hands inviting
Smile crooked

Eyes blurred by the cold
Ears plugged, awaiting a miracle from forgotten songs

A cab appears
Empty

To drive away
  Into another dream
    Into another borough
To drive away
  To another story
    Further up north
      Where a breath can be taken

Before the impending rooster crows
Before light shines again,
The trumpet will sound,
to no ears
The dance will end,
to no applause.

Everything I Know Is a Lie

In the many halls of Borges's library,
You'll find a small nook,
Where my library resides,

It is arranged vertically
Dependent on gravity
...
Rimbaud is burdened by Ethical studies
Nabokov's letters to Vera act as a foundation for one of the pillars

Shelley's buried under Dostoyevsky
Wilhelm Reich is hidden under Garcia

Baudelaire carries Baldwin
Kundera's Novel fights with Hegel's History
Nietzsche is comfortable, Ducasse taunts
Kerouac and Bukowski share a drink and nothing else
Hemingway is everywhere
Faulkner stands alone
...
It is one of many
a speck in infinity
in the ever expanding
Rows and Columns
Making up the totality
of human knowledge and experience

Perpetually
Eternally
Vexingly
Surviving

Lost in the maps of our own making

Empires rising
Kingdoms falling
Republics being erected
Democracies being birthed

Every chant
Every poem
Every song
Every word
Every border
Every -ism
Every god
Every person
Is a lie

The Greatness of Industry
That Unstoppable Human Drive
Keeps eating
Keeps gobbling
Churning
Keeps itself going
Ever consuming
Radiating half-life
Reaping the buried

Let it burn already

Let Quijano wake and Quixote perish
Let him see the world through the eyes of a defeated man
Then let him die already.

Another War to Live Through

Collateral
Approved margins of loss
Statistics
Forced Martyrs
Suffocating yet striving/thriving rats
My people
Are too used to this

Straggled
Remnants
Of tourists
View the weather
On their chipped screens:
Smoke

From pyres
From cigarettes
Cigarillos
Caged ovens
Cigars
Tuned-up raggeded Cars
Illegal Cremations
Cellars that protect from viewing the stars and not the pressures
  of reality
Motors furnacing electric power and Mortician's wages
Neighborhoods occupied by the "imbedded"

Children cry
Play with abandoned wheels
Kick deflated egos with hysteric laughter
Scream and run on all fours
(if they're still whole)

Theaters
Schools

Libraries
Abandoned buildings & doorways
Turned
To orphanages
To En-mass kitchens with the whitest rice
To the refuge of the sea of limbs coming in
On
  Buses
  Vans
  Pick-ups
  Motcykete[1]

-weathered withering faces-

Suspended in Traffic
Birthing and Dying
On cushions made of Asphalts
Between the scratched White & Yellow lines
Beneath a heat not meant for September
Beneath missiles informed of your hearts' desires

The delivery takes too long
The take-way longer
The line at the Butcher's outpaces a live concert's

The Punks still mosh in their pits
The Punks drink their still beers
  Skin glistening from the sweat of percussive movement
    -on beat-
As the tunnels withstand
The damaged and crumbling

The Desert watches on
Waiting for the moment to invest

---

[1] Beat-up motorcycles/ off-brand vespas

The Desert calms her mind
With its mirage

Kid's comic
With its
  harmless humor
Harkens meanings
  As deep & shallow
  As Holy texts
Referenced to validate another
War
Victory
Defeat
-
All of it mundane
-

As interesting as a corpse's wrappings

A man walks through the deserted streets
  His chest embroidered
  With the Silent Scream
  Of unbridled teenage wrath
Eyes used to his alleys
  In every state
Feet memorized by & of every corner

To Pass through the rubble
Where lives went on
To Pass through checkpoints
Erected by impotent armies
To look past newly constructed
  Empty
  Pristine
  Sterilized
Towers

Where bodies fell & flew
Out of windows
Whose glass remains shattered by dreams
  Rummaging
  Scavenging
  Seeking couches
To linger on

Couches long gone
Stained
Overturned
Cushionless
Shipped out
Ravaged by bed bugs
Left on curbs for wandering mutts to piss on
While the Roach watches on
Across manmade craters
Where bricks were made into confetti
To reach him

His body was left intact
His innards shredded
His finger stuck in a populace's mind
His mouth finally shut
His beard remains
His martyrdom finally given by the chosen

The enemy of my enemy
Who is my enemy
Gone
The enemy of my enemy
Who is my enemy
Present

Both their guns are ablaze
Both light up my city's night

Both tango on our tombs
Both usher something endless
Yet final

The laundry is too slow
Too many funerals
Too many graves to visit
Too many images to sacrament
Too many targeted gatherings
  Joining the dead they honour/memorialize
Too many bloodstains to wipe
Too much gravel & dust to beat away

Not enough detergent
Never enough water

The uncaring plants suck in the Sun
The weeds latch on & go up the walls
Reaching the beds of girls
  Whose rushing feet forgot
    Their slippers
    Their blankets
    Their family portraits

The German god-head
Realizes the necessity of war's function in history's making

The American pockets
Realize the necessity of Profit's Margin when opportunity
  is fecund

The Arabs never realize their defeat
Stuck in dried ink
Stuck in fatalism
Stuck in victory's holy prophecy
Never learning

The French are preoccupied with cheese and national identity
And their grammar's integrity

The English take shelter
In the safe and boring

Stalin's Specter's reclaiming Spectral Lands
For the Tsars never left Russian soil

The East is colonizing the African continent

Latin America is busied with its own internal sabotage

Australia is on fire

No one cares about the poles and the melting

A world reeking of
Mundane death
A world seething in
its futility

They Dare
To justify/pacify
Through
Lofty words
Promising Providence

While the rivers of Old
Stream by with blackened tar-like surface
Oozing the scent of cancer
Bubbling with noxious apparitions
To fill the lungs of farmers
To fill the soil with the muck
  Ensuring the dead remain dead
  Obstructing the circle of new life

Ensuring nothing grows
Ensuring the Stoned Angels
Brood over nothing but degraded dust
Their hands clasped by sculptors whose imagination prevents
an opening
Their eyes half-shut for fear of witnessing the stillness of
a rapture where none ascend
A rapture
A damnation
Too dull for any imagined god(s) to enact

There is no glory in
Shells
Blades
Bullets
Bombardments
U.N. Speeches
Bodies
Ligaments
Museum canons

The drones buzzing in a population's ear shot
Too far to shoo away like flies
Near enough to strike like mosquitoes

Behold the cunning carnage of Justified Warfare
Behold the Symphony of raining
Steel
Iron
Circuits

Remember Troy and the Collapsing Bronze Age
Remember Carthage and salted soil
Remember (for years to come) the 10 day siege and massacre
and the accompanying hereditary guilt
Remember Japan's unconditional surrender
and its thermonuclear cost

Remember the Alamo!
Remember '82
Remember '92
Remember 9/11 (yes operator/ I am in danger)
Remember '05 and how it led to '06
Remember '08 the collapse and the 7th May
Remember a Spring that became a Scorching Summer
Remember 2020 (August 4th at the least)
And now remember October 7th and '24
Foresee all the coming Myths dug up from unmarked ditches

It never started
It won't end
It just is

No explosion is surprising
To the ears of a ploughed earth

… … …

The bars are quieter yet still harboring
-they are still docked with their collective strikes-
The prisons are packed, with room for more
-every breath taken is a crime-
The roof's high enough
The basement low enough
To inspire intimacy
-Thanatos begets Eros-

I salute their embrace
  mourn their separation

Expats call and ease their survival's guilt
They pray for the smell of
  cat guts
  dog's spilled entrails

to sense involvement
to appease a conscience
  too taken by Mediterranean Emotional Blackmail
        Bequeathed by a dying Matriarch's limp lips and glassing eyes

It is all quite boring
Loud & annoying
An inconvenience
A headache
Banal even…

A land
A river
minerals
resources
-
not your god
not your existence
not your national pride
not world peace
-
it's nothing but things and the tax for 'em
is the pile of bodies screaming holy verses

it's just
another war to live through

That Good Old Empty Feeling

Warm
    Books
    Blankets
    Hands
Mean nothing to me.

Christmas by
    Lonesome
    Friends
    Family
Seem to pass by
Meaning nothing to me.

As the despicably weak cold
Latches to my lower spine

As my lungs crack
Under the force of my cough

As I get the splitting headaches
Contracting my forehead

It truly means nothing.

As they keep talking of
    Revolutions
    Rights & Wrongs
    Drugs
    Unemployment
    The starving
    The dying
    Bleak futures
It no longer itches my skin.

Planet is heating up
Politicians keep veering towards the right

Fathers are getting older and deader
The dirt is beginning to call my name
But it still doesn't matter.

In Sunshine
In Weathered mornings
Under capitalists or socialists
Behind the scenes or on the forefront
As a joke or serious ponderings

It means nothing.
...
Ideals
Are
Worse
Than
Religions
...
The sanctity of life
Is daily trampled
By Timberlands

The sanctity of death
Is prayed for by murderers
With beads made of mud

The butchers cut the calf and let the blood trickle
The vegans expound their moral high ground

Gluten free
Racially sensitive
Yoga guru
Enlightened beings
Still shit like the rest of us
Still wake in graves

The oblivion from which we came
The oblivion to which we will return
It's that good old empty feeling
Standing, leaning, being, observing neutrally beneath vague ideas
In moments of pensive objectivity

But as I am alive,
As I am still clinging to something,
It becomes harder to turn that blind eye

Unless completely battered
Unless completely out of it

Brain shut off
Memory a haze
Facts chewed up
Dates disorganized
Food puked out
Truly uncaring
Faking no smile nor embrace

A new year is born,
An old one dies,
People celebrate in the streets
People dance on roofs
People kiss tenderly
People fight
Lone persons sit at home
I am in a cab about to undergo the walk between the alleys
  that harbored my upbringing
I am in transition
Lost in indifference,
As it should be.

Capable of loving
Capable of care

Unable to remember
Unable to sustain.

With that endless night
Creeping ever closer
Unnerved by peering brown eyes in the reflections
With that endless night
Promising that deliverance
With that good old empty feeling…

Waiting for a Melody

We are going through the mist,
  Atop a mountain
  Beneath night
  Between gaps & oncoming headlights,
To lose our sight
...
The city is dark below
No one will light a candle

A father toils
On the ever growing machine,
Fingers grinding the letters off their keys

A mother's spine
Is breaking,
Under the weight of smoke

Another mother lies in an overcrowded bed
Her aging heart beating the flooding waters away,
For now...

We keep going through the mist,
  Further & further
  Chasm to our right
  Stone to our left
  Roadkill decorating the coming corner,
To lose our heads
...
The bright brilliant fires of a revolution
Have died out and been reduced to bruises on tarmacs,
For cabbies to complain about

Half is built gloriously and empty
Half is grotesque and full to the brim
With nothing in between

My hole is being filled
No place to hide

My hole is no more
Find somewhere else to die…

We are going through the mist,
  One will keep dealing
  One will keep filming
  One will keep joking
  One will keep talking
  I will keep waiting,
To hear a melody
…

There is no guide for the road ahead
No gas station to shortchange
No stop signs to steal
No point to anything

While the men hold their silence
While the executioners yawn
While negligence explodes in our faces
While the whole damned thing spins into spirals forming patterns
  for historians

I know that halting is a death sentence…

Go through the mist
Lose what you can
Go through the mist
Forget the sacred well
Go through the mist
Abandon your hopes and wait with me
For that eluding melody

A Trumpet Sounds for Another Crawl

In the vast corridors of wind
Came a lone cab
That drove by
Splashing vacant pavements

The first snow has arrived
A dog probably died that night
As lovers passed by
Too preoccupied by
each others' hands

A sound of sirens
  reaches a beggar in the park
    looking for scraps of halal sandwiches
  reaches a neurotic youngster
    sweeping the remnants of tobacco
  reaches a sleeping gal
    too warm under blankets to leave
  reaches two arguing brothers
    under the roof of their upbringing

The fire lights it all up
The tongues of flames enwrap the loners
The black smoke smells of mother's chicken
and
The voice cries out
To a nation of sleepers:
"Look upon the dead
Gaze upon the worms
Face the skulls
Lay a kiss on the disturbed grounds
Climb upon the tombs of ancestors
Wipe thine own sweat
Reach out thine hands
Towards any salvation above

And know it be futile
For judgment has passed"

The whistles sound off the coming trains
The nightskies show the coming planes
The silver knife shows your reflection
A smile will emerge
Eyes will close
Gravity will continue
And a fall
is always
one
push
away

So laugh dear friends
For when we fall
  Let it be after a dance
  Let it be as a song is about to end
  Let it be while we all choke on a joke
  Let it be for another crawl gladly paid in the dawning morning.

Sacred Omens

Lady,
In black,
Guards a parking lot
With fumes of dying cigarette,

As her black dog
Sits on bruised tarmac,
With yellow eyes
That follow passing footsteps,
With tongue out
Panting to the cold wind.

Old man,
Red with exhaustion,
Waters
        weathered sun flowers
                        in flailing grass
In a roundabout
              where cars
                        vans
                             bikes
                                   and foolish hurried feet
Turn madly
            attempting escape.

A group of men
               kick about a ball
                               tackling
                                      bleeding
                                              cursing
                                                    smiling.

A rock erodes away under
                         smoothing rain

Of deranged

out of season

clouds.

A girl itches all over

pukes out

a cheating lover's lies

In a friend's basin.

Boys stare in
Awe
Fear
Mistrust
With belittling smirks,
At a man clad in leather
With eyes hidden under shades
Rushing coolly under
The warm drizzle and misplaced sunshine.

Dark smoke rises above the steeple bells
As the streets are ablaze with discontent.

Shells
Shards
Canisters
Litter the non-beating heart
Of a city.
…
A continent burns
An asteroid approaches
A button is to be pressed
…

The meek hide under shelters
Expecting a promise that won't be met.

The strong duel one another
With
Clubs
Rocks
Rubber
Hands.

They all burn away
In the coming ashes of negligence

They all join the soil
Under the starless blanket

They all take a last breath
Before a last gust of wind

They all welcome
An endless night

Take This Moment

Take this moment
As it passes,

In this second,
A child prays
A student reads
A man oils his gun.

In this second,
I draw breath
In a room with very little light.

Lovers lay fingers on each other
Lone feet trace the pavements with memories
Birds fly in unison above a park.

A sunset is immortalized in a rhyme
A moon inspires lips to join
A soldier burns down his hometown.

You are still in your grave…
Beneath the forgotten fortress…
While others walk with umbrellas under the rain.

A friend pukes in an alley
Another picks a fight
The last one stays home.

A knife is sharpened
A teenager just finished his first novel
A deal is made for lives.

In London, a writer weeps for prisoners
In Berlin, a thinker suffocates under construction
In California, a chemist quantifies Marx

In Turkey, a movie maker feeds a cat
In Brooklyn, a poet reinvents chickpeas
In Beirut, they all eye the plane.

A cigarette is lit
Another is crushed under a heel
Smoke lingers through it all…

Take this moment
Before it passes,
She's leaving towards another's arms
A plane is crashing
He's looking into your eyes
A babe smiles for the first time
She grins at a joke
-
Garbage is collected in a morning
Coffee is spilled in an afternoon
Change is lost behind a counter during a night
-
A car just exploded somewhere
The smoke will rise
The flames will mesmerize
The meat will smell
The sound will deafen
People will die.

A grandfather reads a bedtime story
A grandmother waits patiently in the living room.

A round of cards is dealt
A round of shots is poured
A round bullet is passing through a rib cage.

Take this moment
Lay it on a headstone…

Lay it with a kiss on a forehead…
Lay it tenderly on a pillow…

Take this moment
And stick it in your wallet,
It's all you've got.

We the Beast

We need no avenging gods
No monolithic apparitions
No gaping mouths of manifested oblivion

For beneath
Both the fertile and decimated
There are corpses

The world
Is fed with corpses
Will continue to be fed with corpses
Until it heaves
Dries out
And become one as well

We will play our part
Headlong into mass extinction

In awe
In disgust
With righteous fury
With non-sequitur sounds
In orchestral operas
In silent walks
In full protest
In negligent neutrality
Armed with apathy
Crowned with ignorance
Proclaiming full knowledge

We will usher in
The age of none
In the name of all

I wake
Hearing the cries of babes
From the neighbor's house

I wake
To my cough
To the smoke I must exhale
To a dancing figure, spinning statically, above my coffee grinds

I wake
Once more
To take part
In the drudgery
In the commute between here and there
In the acts that move the hands ticking away

I wake longing to sleep again
I wake to the urge to numb myself again
I wake to a single pillow accumulating my fallen hair, in a room accumulating dust

We the beast
Are hungry
Though surrounded with flesh

We the beast
Are itching
Though overly compensated with distractions

We the beast
Are bored.
Longing for epics
Aching for intrinsic purpose

We dream of annihilation
Contend with domestication
Allow ourselves illusions of grandeur

Mongrels chasing after our own tail
Alpha and Omega
We pretend

Signs are given matter
By those desperate for patterns

Grandmothers across the world knit sweaters with patterns
Scientists drone on over scopes studying patterns
Writers rhyme for the sake of patterns
Economists read patterns

The only constant
The only certainty
Is entropy

The futility in the face of it
The fear of succumbing to it
The ache to reach it

We will reach it

As a lone rider laughs
In his mad journey

As the sole survivor weeps
Through gouged eyes

As existence keeps spinning statically
Above the coffee grinds of perpetuality
Till it too dissolves into a cup
To be enjoyed momentarily
Accompanied
By a song
By a smoke
By a dawning

That will also be
Extinguished
In favor of
An endless night with…
 No bums to loiter in
 No moon for hounds to howl at
 No lovers to distil its fragrance
 No eyes to immortalize it
 No beasts to slumber through it.

To the Descent

A bomb descends…

in a street
someone got mugged

in a house
someone got raped

in a school
a shooting commences

in an office
a robbery is being committed via email

in a house of power
the ones in charge stroke themselves

A bomb descends…

Over a bridge
A couple interlocks lips

Inside a bar
Old friends reconnect

On a battlefield
A life is saved for another day

In an abandoned parking lot
Children play their sports and games

A bomb descends…
Above…
  the dying
  the living

those to come
those that are buried

Above…

Lovers of words
Killers of sounds
Mothers of the wayward
Teachers of obedience and math
Crooks behind smiles
Dealers of salvations
Blindmen in hallways
Cutters of meats
Preachers of endings
Butchers of lambs
Beaters of skulls
Surgeons of the throatless

Above
A lone rider
A lone rider driving
Forward on the open stretch towards oblivion leaving the tracks
that shadow a momentary connection with the road crossed
and to pave the one ahead in the futile exhilarating frustrating
engine-pumping rush of living while hearing the descent

A bomb descends
A lone rider laughs.

Endless Night

Within folding cities,
Temporary people sang
Preceding the coming fires,
Temporary people held each other
Preceding the coming winds.

I, lie awake
Anticipating

We, now lie still
In the aftermath.

Three women
Whom I loved
Are preserved on the walls
In the alleys where suicide is a mercy

Their eyes erased
Their gaze engraved
In the memories
Of all who are gone.

All greenery is gone.
All breathers have disappeared.

Bricks
Blocks
Granite
Metal
The Mausoleum
Meant for my eyes,
The inheritance for a world
Where my whisper reaches no ears
Nor escapes my mouth.

No loud laughter
Nor solemn cries
In subway carts.

No mountain climbers
To invade rooftop festivities.

No carpenters
To construct the library
Housing incomplete knowledge.

No lone rover
To drive with speed
Across vacant highways
Dedicated to the habitual sacrifice of rodents.

The cabs
Have rusted away,
Along with the coming passengers.

Billie's songs
Are played no more.

The moon is alone
Without the kiss
To celebrate its presence
Without the howl
To mark courageous forgotten acts.

A submarine lies,
All hollowed out,
On the tip of a hill
eroding away.

Nothing is left
To inhale

Any perfume
Or the products
Of exhaust pipes.

Nothing is left
To hear
The still ringing echoes
Of a world gone dark,
Blessed by endless night...

With no east for a rising
With no west for a setting
With no north nor south
With no reason to know any which way;
An equalizer bringing silence

For no soul to sleep in
No mind to dream it away
No hands to clutch it
No feet to stumble across it...

With no rain to muddy the sands nor overflow calcified sewers
With no cries to flap the balcony's curtains nor carry grounded
grinded birds

Endless night
Of my childhood dreams,
Endless night
Of the preacher's warnings,

Eradicator of
All who worshiped your refuge & shunned it,
Mother of
All violent acts,
Friend and keeper of secrets
For both lovers and killers,

You have buried us
In your embrace.

For no sole survivor
  should exist
No singular face
  should encompass
    a whole civilization
No heart
  should experience
    the weight of the stillness
No sentience
  should have the misfortune
    To comprehend the combined corpses of all ages
      Decomposing in scorched forests
        Festering in uninhabited city streets
          Hanging from the lips
            Of broken statutes
              Dangling with
                no air to blow them away
                no fire to finish the job,
No being
  should strive
    to find the remnants
      of a world under the cloak
        of my endless night.

Sole Survivor

I am the one that lost a lung on the tracks
The one that slipped on the tarmac of highways
I have reached heights in your annals of academia
I have breached the bottoms of your bottles
I've rummaged through your trash for a sentence
Saw a deity in the aisles of a nearby deli
Read the numbers scrawled on toiletries
Ate through the layers of fat

I have heard the coming bombs
I have inhaled the toxins
I have seen the stray bullets
I have eyed down the squirrels
I have felt every bruise on my limbs
I have endured the heat of too many summers
I have tasted the stale in hours of need

At times
All that you can manage
Is but a raised hand
To shoot down
Numb-ers

At times
All that you can stomach
Is a fading smile

All I can do
Is laugh maniacally
Is drink a few more
Is smoke till ashes rule
Is to love for at least a moment

In doomed parades
In dimmed basements

On rooftops dedicated to flights
On rotten wooden tables missing a leg
In the middle of city streets awaiting our refuge

Join me
whomever
is left

Share with me
this stillness of
a sleeping world,

for I cannot bear it.

To Dig a Grave for the World

Church bells toil no more
Mosques proclaim no time of piety
Temples admit no wandering tourists
Butcher shops have no more meat to chop
Love has been weeded out of brothels
Taverns are dry

The swing set has no one to push
Its saddle in the dirt where grass once grew
Its metal rusted/fractured
No one screams
Joy

Brooklyn
-in its infinite wisdom-
Is preserved
In the December morning
When petrified eyes are laid at its solitude
-No feet trouble pavements-

The shovel rests
No longer giving splinters to callous hands
No longer breathing space into the ground

The world digs its own grave
Under the blanket of an endless night
Void of dates
Void of epitaphs
void of dreams.

The Old Roach Knows

Before the Lizards fossilized
After comets reshaped maps
…
The Old Roach was around
…
Before sticks were sharpened
Before stones were kneeled to
Before trees were processed

While the floor was lava
While the world was an aquarium
After wheels and cogs made bicycles and can-openers
After gunfire was placed in museums
…
The Old Roach remained
…
Before ports were erected
With ships adorned with sails of pillaging and commerce
Before beer was fermented and Gods were assigned to its distillation

After cyanide was introduced into fillings
After cylindrical Metal became the 5th season just before the fall
After eyes were sent out beyond stratospheres and privacy eliminated
…
The Old Roach kept vigil
…
While words came and went
Into and out of graves
From the tops of Pyramids
  Swallowed up by fauna and sand
  Uncovered by curious and greedy hands
To the lowest crevice of developing sewages
  Being fed indigested corn, blood, tampons, coffee grinds, and
    the cinders of Alexandria
  Slowly streaming past remnants of forgotten ancestors

…
The Old Roach
Listened and read
Secret and Public records
…
Before NYC
Before London
Before Florence
Before Paris
Before Al-Kaaba
Before the Vatican
Before Jerusalem
Before Rome & Carthage and the sacking of Troy
Before the first oars went across the two sanctified rivers
Before the first Alphabet and After the last incomprehensible
screech
…
The Old Roach will witness
…
Out of the cold womb
Of a careless mother
Of empty spaces
Of Endless Night
Enveloping all that was and is to come

Into the merciless heat
Of Thermonuclear celebration
Of the saunafication of a globe
Of Inevitable Dawns
Birthing matter with fire
…
The Old Roach will have his corner
…
Nibbling at the feet of the martyrs' rotten corpses
Coronating the heads of prideful fleeting rats
…

The Old Roach
Has seen
Every petal form

Has heard
Every extinct whimper

Has tasted
Every scrap across culinary ages

Has caressed
All unfolding histories

Has smelled
Every convenient lie being flushed

Has felt every
Boot
Poison
Broom
Bullet
Pellet
Fist
Tissue
Tooth
Radiation
And resumed
…
The Old Roach knows
No cause to scream
No cause to live
No cause to die
No cause to write
…
The Old Roach
Simply Knows.

Inevitable Dawn

A sound
A rhythm
A band
An orchestra
Heaven's cacophony
-A melody-
It rises

Light appears
Light is extending
Bright new furnace
Bright new chariot

Dawn is arriving

The engines of matter
Kick in
Movement
Force
Time
Ignition
Revving

Soon…
Cemetery will turn to garden
Nebulas will turn
Harmonicas will be picked up

Soon…
Will come
The Angel
My wife and his lover
The one with the library
The Sun Kissed Blue Eyed Man and the One with
  the Strongest Glasses

The Man who is my enemy in name alone
The Cop Slayer
The Refugee and her lover
The May Queen
The Good Man
Old Faces I had forgotten
Old Faces I had missed
Old Faces that had changed for better or worse
Benjamin the Wise
The Prophet
The Lady
Mary Jane

Different names
Different faces
Traced by the old
New as the dawning
………..
The certainty of dusk
Brings forth
The inevitability of dawn
………..

The lone tree
Looming
Ashen white
Branchless
Faceless

Towers
Above
The Dawning

Blocks
Its ambassadors
From reaching

The rubbled
Parking lots

The lone tree
Marks the land

The dark will not abide
Stubborn to the last shadow
Every minion called upon
Every general of war
Every front line grunt
Every rester in the abyss
Weapons held
Breath held
Eyes redshot
Teeth hidden

The bright washes over
No stopping a tide
No stopping inevitability

That which withers
Sustains anew

Out of every corpse
New grass

our dove
remains buried
beneath the roots
New fossils

Soon…
Breaking
Rolling
Burning

Puffing
Inhaling
Passing
Drowning
Exhaling
Eating
Fucking
Warring
Thieving
Thinking
Dooming

Soon…
Loving
Playing
Singing
Nurturing
Building
Creating
Feeling
Blossoming

Soon…
A babe
Holding mother's hair

Alpha
smiles
no care

Alpha
Harbinger of new beginnings

Apollo
Has risen
Victory has come

Victory has come
Ring the new found bells
Victory is here

Insufferable Noon

Stuck in high heaven
Needle's pointing high-noon
Bathing all
Drenching all
The work continues
Hot breath must come out
The work continues
Numbers must be misplaced
The work continues
melodies are being drowned out
the bells have become deafening
And on it goes
Streets must be colored
And on it goes
Streets are now fading into burning white
And on it goes
Everything under the Sun
Will keep spinning
Will twirl to the strings
Everything under the Sun
Stuck under high heaven
Sweating through their vision
Toiling away any thought
Toiling away the other hours of the day
Toiling away in the hopes of invoking
Another night
To caress away all the colors being washed away by the heat
Toiling away in the hopes of invoking
The Night
Carrying the dreams to soothe away the price
Carrying the breeze that stabs me with a toothpick
Carrying me away from this insufferable noon

Invoking Night

Be the deaf singer
Wearing soft-soled shoes
Allowing the imprint of vibrations
To direct the notes emerging from throat and gut

Be the flower seller
That drops the petals into pockets
Running as deep as dried puddles
Directing the coming feet

Be the moon
Ever shadowed/Ever present
Be my moon
The constant companion

Be the wingless pilot
With the last and only prayer
Invoking the soothing night

"Drown out the hum
With your quietude

Smear overwhelmed visions
With ignorable shades
With damning trailing steps

Bludgeon the electric eye
Steal the signs and their paths
Give unto me a moment's rest"

A pin drops
The neighborhood rings
A light is shed
The dark resumes
Shielding exposed retinas,
Till the inevitable dawning…

To Yet Another Dawn

There was no great song
There was no dance for the ages

The streets were tame
The people fearful
The sky dry

Aragon's women skirted by
As Hemingway's men limped to their stools

The air is still poison

The architect found fertile soils abroad
The poet is losing himself in monsters and men
The actor lived out her last night couched away
The lover hides in the hospital bed
The writer sends another letter despite herself
The farmer will rescue another dog by the sea
The librarian finds yet another book to catalogue
...
It keeps going
Blood runs
Words ring
Water flows
Memory fades
It keeps going
...
And all the
Coffee makers
Van drivers
Hair cutters
Fruit peddlers
Trash sifters
Perfume hustlers
Tarmac lickers

Money counters
Lovers of Life & Dwellers of Graves
Gave a sigh

To the night bearing a new dawn
That none want to see coming

Pillow's Defense

Faces crash on the waves
Faces surround
Eyes of mothers
Brow of patriarch
Lucky tooth, lucky grin

Around the corner
They wait for me
Behind the fuse box blocking the street
They electrify city air

Faces plunge on couches
Faces of gods peered out of grayed bricks
For them to witness a dance
Heads of the gone rose from beneath dusted carpet
For all to be mourned

Faces surround
Feel it
From the pavement-spitting lips furnacing industry
From the sniffing of lottery sellers
From the weight carried by wandering eyes
Feel
The passing & the coming
The familiar & The deceiver
The memory & the present

Keep your lids shut
Keep your breath toxic
Keep the coffee for later

Faces
Retire
Behind
Pillow

About the Author

Assem Bazzi is a Lebanese poet who has been contributing to the Beirut poetry performance scene since the summer of 2011. Performing in street corners, local bars, and the occasional theater stages, he has participated in numerous poetry events, including ones curated by The Poetry Pot, Poetic License, Pen Lebanon, and Haven for Artists. Bazzi is also a founding member of el-Yafta poetry circle. He has contributed to the literary travel guide book *Beirut Guide for Beirutis*, and has a poetry book published by Barzakh titled *From Martyr to Rat*.

www.ingramcontent.com/pod-product-compliance
Lightning Source LLC
LaVergne TN
LVHW050942080826
845145LV00004B/1367